W9-BGK-246

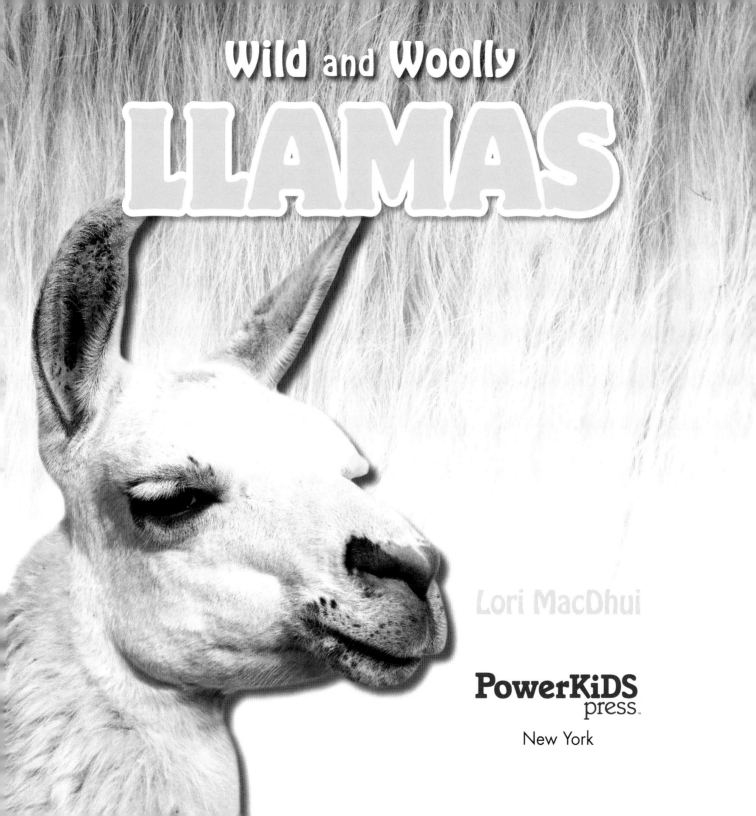

Wild and Woolly
LLAMAS

Lori MacDhui

PowerKiDS
press.

New York

Published in 2018 by The Rosen Publishing Group, Inc.
29 East 21st Street, New York, NY 10010

First Edition

Editor: Theresa Morlock
Book Design: Rachel Rising

Photo Credits: Cover, p. 1 a_v_d/Shutterstock.com; Cover (background) espiegle/ E+/Getty Images; Cover, pp. 1, 3, 4, 6, 8, 10, 12, 14, 16, 18, 20, 22, 23 iStockphoto.com/Whiteway; p. 4 Dmitry Burlakov/Shutterstock.com; p. 5 Bartosz Hadyniak/E+/Getty Images; pp. 6, 22 Eric Isselee/Shutterstock.com; p. 7 (llama) Toniflap/Shutterstock.com; p. 7 (vicuña) Stefano Buttafoco/Shutterstock.com; p. 7 (alpaca) pickypalla/Shutterstock.com; p. 7 (guanaco) Anton_Ivanov/Shutterstock.com; p. 8 iStockphoto.com/lauriek; p. 9 aaabbbccc/Shutterstock.com; p.11 hadynyah/E+/Getty Images; p. 12 Lenor Ko/Shutterstock.com; p. 13 SC Image/Shutterstock.com; p. 15 Janet Horton/Alamy Stock Photo; p. 16 Aksenova Natalya/Shutterstock.com; p. 17 amadeustx/Shutterstock.com; p. 18 Josh Cornish/Shutterstock.com; p. 19 Amy Johansson/Shutterstock.com; p. 20 David Gaylor/Shutterstock.com; p. 21 andresr/ E+/Getty Images.

Cataloging-in-Publication Data

Names: MacDhui, Lori.
Title: Llamas / Lori MacDhui.
Description: New York : PowerKids Press, 2018. | Series: Wild and woolly | Includes index.
Identifiers: ISBN 9781538326015 (pbk.) | ISBN 9781538325315 (library bound) | ISBN 9781538326022 (6 pack)
Subjects: LCSH: Llamas–Juvenile literature.
Classification: LCC QL737.U54 M238 2018 | DDC 599.63'67–dc23

Manufactured in the United States of America

CPSIA Compliance Information: Batch #BW18PK: For Further Information contact Rosen Publishing, New York, New York at 1-800-237-9932

CONTENTS

Meet the Llama!

Llamas are unusual creatures. Their bodies are narrow and their legs and necks are long. Their heads are small and their ears are large. Their funny-looking teeth seem to stick out.

Based on a llama's looks, you might not think it seems very useful. But did you know that llamas have been working with people for thousands of years? Llamas are sturdy pack animals, able to carry heavy loads over rocky land. They're also **fiber** animals—their wool can be made into warm, long-lasting cloth.

Most llama herds are kept by people living in Bolivia, Peru, Ecuador, Chile, and Argentina.

5

A Camel's Cousin

Llamas are part of the Camelidae family. The Camelidae family is broken into two groups: Camelini and Lamini. The Camelini group includes Bactrian and Arabian camels. The Lamini group includes llamas, alpacas, guanacos, and vicuñas.

How can a llama in South America be related to a camel in Africa? Scientists believe that the early members of the Camelidae family lived in North America. These animals traveled to South America and Asia over land bridges and died out in North America. Today's llamas and camels **evolved** from the animals that survived.

Llamas are the biggest and tallest of the four Lamini **species**.

llama

guanaco

alpaca

vicuña

7

Llama Characteristics

Llamas are about 47 inches (119.4 cm) tall at the shoulder. They weigh around 250 pounds (113.4 kg). Although they're large, llamas are herbivores. That means they only eat plants. They're able to survive on many different kinds of plants and don't need very much water.

Llamas have special **adaptations** that help them survive high in their mountain homes. Their feet have two toes and wide pads on the bottom that help them walk on rocky land.

llama foot ←

Fuzzy Features

Llamas can live for up to 20 years.

Llamas' thick coats keep them warm in the windy mountains.

Beasts of Burden

More than 5,000 years ago, people living in the Andes Mountains **domesticated** llamas. Since that time, they've used llamas to carry supplies and people across the mountainous landscape.

Llamas can carry loads of 50 to 75 pounds (22.7 to 34 kg) for up to 20 miles (32.2 km) in a day. If a llama feels that its load is too heavy, it may refuse to move. Llamas have been known to spit or kick at their owners until their pack is made lighter.

Fuzzy Features

Domesticated llamas evolved from wild guanacos.

This Quechua Indian woman is shown standing with her llama in Cuzco, Peru.

Many Uses

Llamas were very important to the Inca civilization. The Incas used llamas as a source of food, **fuel**, and clothing. Today, people continue to use llamas in many ways. Llama waste can be burned as fuel. Their hides can be used to make leather. Llamas are also kept for their meat. Perhaps most importantly, llamas are kept for their wool, which can be made into clothing, rugs, and rope. Llama fiber is warm and strong.

← llama wool scarf

Fuzzy Features

Llamas were so important to the Inca that llama statues were often buried with their dead.

This llama is standing in the Inca city of Machu Picchu in Peru. Machu Picchu was built during the 1400s and still stands today.

13

Llama Fiber

A llama's coat has two layers—a **coarse** outer layer and a soft under layer. The outer layer is made of tough hairs called guard hairs. The undercoat is made of short, soft, wavy hairs. To collect the fiber, llama owners must shear, or cut off, this coat every two years or so.

The shearing process requires teamwork. Two people hold the llama steady while one person removes its hair. Don't worry, shearing doesn't hurt llamas! They're simply held down so they don't get cut accidentally.

Fuzzy Features

Llamas that produce the best fiber are often chosen for **breeding.**

Today, shearing is often done using electric **razors**. The llama pictured here is tied in a stall to keep it still during shearing.

15

Processing the Fiber

A llama can produce about 6.6 pounds (3 kg) of fiber in one shearing. After the fiber is sheared, it's cleaned and sorted. The guard hairs make up about 20 percent of the total fiber. These hairs are longer than the soft hairs and are less **valuable**. Separating the coarse guard hairs from the soft hairs is called dehairing.

Spinning is the process by which fiber is made into yarn. Llama fiber is spun into yarn, then woven or knitted into cloth.

← spinning wheel

Fuzzy Features

Llama fiber comes in many shades of white, gray, brown, red, and black.

Llama yarn is often dyed bright, eye-catching colors.

17

Llama Behaviors

Llamas are gentle creatures. They're easy to handle and get along well with people. Llamas can be trained to perform simple tasks.

Llamas are happiest living in groups called herds. They **communicate** with each other through sounds and by moving their ears and tails. Llamas hum when they're worried or uncomfortable. They cluck when they're meeting a new llama. When they sense danger, llamas will let out a high-pitched cry. This warns the rest of the herd to run away.

A baby llama is called a *cria*.

19

Livestock or Pets?

Llamas are livestock, or farm animals. Some farmers keep llamas as guard animals. For example, a llama might be kept with a herd of sheep. Since the llama is taller, it can spot predators and warn the herd.

Some people also keep llamas as pets. In the United States, llamas are now also used as therapy animals. A therapy animal's job is to offer people comfort. Therapy llamas visit nursing homes and hospitals so that people can pet them and feel happy.

Llamas are often kept in petting zoos. They're gentle and safe for children to pet and sometimes ride.

Lovely Llamas

Llamas are very useful animals. They can carry heavy loads, produce fiber for cloth, guard herds of sheep, and provide comfort and companionship to people. Llamas' mild natures and adaptability make them valuable both as livestock and as pets.

Historically, llamas have been an important part of life in the Andes Mountains. Although they've been common in South America for thousands of years, they're just beginning to grow in popularity in the United States. Our relationship with these funny-faced creatures has only just begun!

GLOSSARY

adaptation: A change in a living thing that helps it live better in its habitat.

breed: To bring a male and female animal together so they will have babies.

coarse: Rough or wiry.

communicate: To share ideas and feelings through sounds and motions.

domesticate: To breed and raise an animal for use by people.

evolve: To grow and change over time.

fiber: A long, thin thread, such as animal hair or fur, that can be used to make cloth.

fuel: Something used to make energy, warmth, or power.

razor: A tool with a sharp blade used to remove hair.

species: A group of plants or animals that are all the same kind.

valuable: Important or worth money.

INDEX

WEBSITES

Due to the changing nature of Internet links, PowerKids Press has developed an online list of websites related to the subject of this book. This site is updated regularly. Please use this link to access the list: www.powerkidslinks.com/wandw/llama